SOLOMON SIRE
AND THE
FANTASTIC FIB

Diane E. Root

Illustrated by
Priscilla Alpaugh

The World of
SOLOMON SIRE
Character–Building Fun for Young Children

Copyright © 2012 by Diane E. Root
All rights reserved. No part of this publication may be reproduced, stored in a retrieval system
or transmitted in any form or by any means, electronic, mechanical, photocopying, recording or
otherwise, without written permission of the publisher.

ISBN: 978-0-9859286-0-5 (hard cover)
ISBN: 978-0-9859286-1-2 (ebook)
Library of Congress Control Number: 2012917109

Published by Solomon Sire Ventures
9 Joslin Lane, Southborough, MA 01772 USA
www.solomonsire.com

Manufactured in the USA

CPSIA Compliance Information: Batch #11/2012. For further information contact RJ Communications,
NY NY, 800-621-2556.

Book design by Jill Ronsley, www.suneditwrite.com

To my wonderful husband, DJ, who believed from the start.
Carrying it forward in honor of C. G. W. Sr.
—Diane E. Root

To everyone who ever believed in me, especially David, Tim and Addie.
—Priscilla Alpaugh

I'm Solomon Sire,
a regular mouse,
who lives, just like you,
on a street in a house.

With Mom, Dad and Sis
we're a family of four.
Nothing so special, I thought,
but no more!

It all really started
the day that I found
an amazing old box,
with strange symbols all around ...

I found it that day on a low closet rack,
surrounded by clothes and pushed way in the back.

It looked big and heavy, but didn't have locks,
just strange golden markings all over the box.

I wondered and wondered...what could this box be?
Then Dad wandered in and he sat down with me.

He said, "You've found our Great Box, I can see.
Inside it are gems, quite a few earned by me.

It's been in our family forever, my dear,
each of us facing its tests, year by year.

And now it's your turn! You will be the next one
to master our family's Great Box, my dear son!

Choose one of the symbols, and rub it like so.
Your journey begins when the mark starts to glow."

I stared at the Great Box and then picked a sign.
I rubbed and I rubbed 'til it started to shine!

"The Fantastic Fib, that's an interesting choice,"
said Dad with a low, thoughtful tone in his voice.

"To master the Fib is quite tough, I would say.
I can't wait to hear all about it one day."

And then he got up and walked quickly away.

Well ...

The next day at school after lunchtime was through,
my friends were all boasting 'bout things they could do.

"I'll bet I can jump to that hydrant," said Matt.
I looked at my legs and thought, "Could I do that?"

"Oh, that's no big deal," said my other friend Pete.
"I'll bet I can leap to that tall park bench seat."

"I'm sure that my jump will be furthest of all—
right over that see-saw," said my friend Big Paul.

Next it was my turn. They all looked at me,
then down at my legs, as short as can be.

I had to say something to make them agree
that I was as good—no, much better! They'd see!

"I'll jump up that flag pole right there!" I cried out.
But then I felt something POP out of my mouth!

It spun on the ground. No one saw it but me,
but I knew for sure what it was instantly ...

A FANTASTIC FIB!

A Fantastic Fib had plunked right on the lawn!
I wasn't sure what to do, so I went on.

"Oh, yes!" I said, "Yes, that is what I can do.
 I'll jump to the top of that flag pole. Can you?"

Their eyes opened wide. My friends all shook their heads.
Then Matt said, "Don't tell us. Just show us instead."

UH-OH!

"Um ... well ..." I said quickly, "things must be just so.
A jump of this size is not easy, you know.

I'll need a full tummy to make this jump right,
and since lunch is finished there's no food in sight.

I guess I won't jump up the flag pole today."
I turned and I walked very quickly away.

I secretly hoped they'd forget the next day.

And what of that Fib? Well, it followed me home!
In fact, it looked larger...I think it had grown.

The next day at school after finishing lunch,
I passed all my friends, sitting down in a bunch.

Pete said, "It is time for your pole-jumping show!
Your tummy is full, so now, up, up you go!"

"Oh...well," I thought quickly, "there's really no way.
You see, I'm not wearing my sneakers today.

I need my red sneakers to jump up that high
so, no pole today! See you later! Bye bye!"

I rushed to my seat, glad to just get away.
That Fib, though, was growing much bigger each day.

The next afternoon at a quarter to three,
my friends and I gathered for gym class. Yippee!

"Hey look!" Pete said, pointing, "Those shoes on your feet!
I see bright red sneakers laced up nice and neat.

We just finished lunch so you must show us how
you'll make your big jump. Please, come show us right now!"

I had to think hard. But, what could I say?
"What day is it now?" I asked, "Oh, it's Wednesday?
Well, Thursdays are really the very best day..."

"And Thursday's tomorrow!" cried my friend Big Paul.
"Tomorrow's the day when you'll show one and all

Just how you can do that gigantic a feat?
Hooray! We can't wait! It will be a great treat."

That night in my room as I sat in my bed,
that Fib would not stop swirling all 'round my head.

I thought, "What an awful mess I'm in today.
I wish the whole thing would just please go away!"

I then heard Mom's voice as she stood at my door.
"Did you know I once faced that same Fib before?

The Fib does get out of control, there's no doubt,
so here is a tip: the truth snuffs the Fib out."

The next day I walked up to school and—SURPRISE!
I really just could not believe my own eyes!

There were my friends, all waiting for me,
with classmates, and teachers, and Principal Blee!

And there was the barber! The fireman named Ned!
The grocery store owner and old Dr. Fred!

In fact, the whole town had come out just to see
someone jump way up the flag pole—ME!

Then what happened next? That big Fib blasted in!
But now it was HUGE—a wild, powerful wind!

I grabbed and held tight to the towering pole
but the Fib was so strong, it was out of control!

And just as I couldn't hold on anymore,
I thought of Mom's words from the dark night before.

And all of a sudden, I knew what to do.
I took a deep breath, and I counted, "One ... two ..."
and yelled just as loud as I could, "IT'S NOT TRUE!

I really can't jump up this flag pole today,
not even with sneakers or lunch on Thursday.

I knew I could not make that jump, but, you see,
I said that so you would think highly of me."

The next thing I heard was a whirling WHOOSH sound.
And then, it was silent. I looked all around.

That Fib—it was gone. Not a trace anywhere.
All that remained was me, just sitting there...

...and a large purple gem sparkling bright in the air.

The crowd started leaving, still looking at me,
and I felt so foolish, and small as could be.

"Aw, Solomon," said Matt and Pete, "it's all right.
Yes, seeing you jump would have been quite a sight.

But we like you, Solomon, just as you are.
Who cares that you really can't jump all that far?"

That night after dinner I told Mom and Dad
about the huge Fib and the big day I'd had.

"You've passed a great test!" said my dad, happily.
"You're well on your way in this journey, I see."

I placed my new gem with those I'd seen before,
and wondered what else that Great Box had in store.

But one thing's for sure. I have now come to see
there IS something special in my family!

Thinking It Through with Solomon

A Parent's Guide for Continuing the Conversation

1. In this story, Solomon told his friends a fib. People sometimes tell fibs because they don't want to get into trouble, or don't want to be embarrassed or they want to make themselves feel better. Why do you think Solomon told a fib about jumping so high?

2. Telling a fib can make us feel uncomfortable or nervous, and might make us do and say strange things. Did Solomon do or say anything strange that gave his friends a clue that he was fibbing?

3. When someone tells a lot of fibs, it makes people nervous about trusting that person. What might Solomon's friends think the next time he tries to tell them something?

4. It can take a lot of courage to go back and tell the truth after we have fibbed. How did Solomon make the fib go away? What could Solomon have said instead of telling a fib in the first place?

5. Sometimes people tell fibs called "white lies" in order to not hurt someone's feelings. For example, you might tell your grandmother you like her cookies so you don't hurt her feelings, even though you really don't like them. Is it OK to tell a "white lie"? What could you say instead to avoid hurting someone's feelings?

6. Can you think of an example in your family when someone fibbed? What happened? How did things turn out in the end?

About This Series

This book is the first in a series of *The Adventures of Solomon Sire* stories which were developed to give parents a fun, easy way to talk to their young children about concepts of character. By making abstract ideas more concrete for children, these stories provide both an engaging starting place for dialog and a context for continued conversation that help parents introduce and reinforce qualities of character in their families.

Look for these upcoming *Adventures of Solomon Sire*:

Solomon Sire and the Chant of I-Can't
Solomon Sire and the Big Bully
Solomon Sire in a Huge Hurry
Solomon Sire and the Great Show of Kindness

About the Author

Diane E. Root created *The Adventures of Solomon Sire* to help introduce concepts of character to her own children. She is the founder of Solomon Sire Ventures (www.solomonsire.com), a company offering books, classes and materials that make character development fun for young children and their families. Diane lives in Southborough, Massachusetts, with her husband and their boy-girl twins.

About the Illustrator

Priscilla Alpaugh has been creating illustrations, paintings, animations, and murals in her studio at Artspace in Maynard, Massachusetts since 2001. A graduate of The University of Massachusetts, Amherst with a BFA in Painting and Illustration, Priscilla also attended Syracuse University's ISDP MFA Illustration program. She is a member of the Society of Children's Book Writers and Illustrators and the Greater Boston Illustrator's Group. Priscilla lives in Maynard, Massachusetts with her husband, son, and daughter. You can see more of her work at www.priscillaalpaugh.com.